DEDICATION

Years ago just before I took the bar exam my life was turned upside down when my mother was killed in a car accident.

I dedicate this book to her and all whose lives have been turned upside down in a motor vehicle accident.

7 Highly Effective Steps To Get The Money You Deserve

When You've Been Badly Injured in a Kansas Car Accident

Paul D. Hogan

ISBN-10: 069226504X
ISBN-13: 978-0692265048 (Paul D. Hogan)

Legal Crusher

(Disclaimer, denial, negation, abjuration and repudiation)

This book is written to provide basic general information which is easily and readily available from public sources such as the internet.

It is provided with the understanding that the author is *not* providing legal advice nor is an attorney client relationship established, in any manner, actual or implied.

Please recognize laws can be changed by court decisions and legislative bodies. The procedures, process and ideas expressed are illustrative and not guarantees of any outcome.

If legal assistance may be required then the services of a licensed attorney should be sought.

CONTENTS

PREFACE

Some people are of the opinion when *you* suffer an injury it is minor; when *they've* suffered an injury it is a bad injury, no matter what.

Let me qualify what a bad injury is:

1. Admitted into the hospital for treatment.
2. Suffered broken bones, especially if it's weight bearing.
3. Undergone a surgical procedure.
4. Sustained visible, substantial scarring.
5. Incurred $10,000 in medical treatment compared to Diagnostic Testing (MRI, X-rays, CT Scans)
6. Suffered a permanent injury requiring ongoing treatment.

INTRODUCTION

I'm going to share with you exactly how to get your car repaired or replaced if it's been totaled, how to get your medical bills paid, and how to obtain reimbursement for your wage loss. When we're done, you're not going to have to worry about whether or not you've taken the right steps. These are the right steps to take. The information I'm about to give you can save you time and weeks or months of frustration.

Some people may be suspicious about getting information from an attorney like this. During my close to forty years of practice I've heard the jokes, I've heard all the statements about lawyers, and here's why I'm giving you this information, bluntly, I don't like to see people screwed by big insurance companies.

Just yesterday, the day before I wrote this, I received a phone call from a man in Dodge City. I learned that he had been involved in a car accident. He was a passenger in a car that had been struck by another car, which ran the red light. His injuries caused him to be transported by EMS to the hospital, where he was admitted. He was treated and the next day he was discharged and ordered to follow up with his family doctor, which he did.

In the meantime, the insurance company for the bad driver contacted him and offered him five hundred dollars. He accepted their offer and signed a release which meant he could not make further claim for the money even if he needed more medical treatment. This was a big, huge mistake, and I wish he would have called an attorney to find out his options before he made that mistake.

Just before I became an attorney, the month before I took the Bar Exam, my life was turned upside down when my mother was killed in a car wreck. Now I try to help other people whose lives have been turned upside down because of car accidents. After I became a lawyer, I spent twenty years trying cases, and I became a pretty good trial lawyer. Then I started advertising and developed a niche practice … and by niche practice I mean I only accepted car accident cases. Because of advertising, lots of people called for help.

We opened lots and lots of cases. The challenge became how to move these cases to a fast settlement for each of our clients. We tried different methods. We would assign an attorney and a paralegal, which is the classic operation in most law offices, to handle a case. Sometimes, cases didn't get moved as fast as I thought they should. Then I tried departments, putting a team of people in one department to move a case from that department to the next. Still, the ball got dropped, and sometimes it was like, when raising kids, I had asked why the ball got dropped, or who dropped the ball, and it was "not me, not me."

I hired more attorneys and more paralegals. We worked hard, but we still struggled with efficiently moving cases to the fast settlement that our clients wanted. Going through this process of handling thousands of cases over the years, I discovered the secret, and I created a process, a system. This resulted in a dramatic change in the speed with which I moved a case to obtain that fast settlement for my client. We were more efficient in how we handled the case and got the information. This took thirty-five years, and talking to ten thousand people injured in a car wreck, much like yourself. Now, with the system, I'm able to give clients information about the fast action that I've taken on their case. Frankly, that's been a great benefit to me because by giving this information to my clients, it cut down drastically on telephone calls from the clients, asking what the status of their case was.

Clients received information from me where I could show them the steps that we took, and the fear of the unknown was eliminated as we guided them step by step through this process of moving a case to a fast settlement. Giving them and showing them the information was especially important for those who had never been involved in a car wreck before. With a system, I was able to get the medical bills paid, and I was able to obtain reimbursement for the wage loss suffered by my client.

Here is the single most important piece of information I can give you. The bad driver who caused this accident, his insurance carrier, is going to make one payment to you, one time, and that's for all your losses; your medical expense, your wage loss, both past and in the future, your pain and suffering, the inconvenience, the hassle; all these elements of losses. They will make one payment to you, one time.

That's when you sign a release, saying that you're not going to make a claim for one penny more. Now, let me back up. They will first pay you your property damage claim, which is separate and apart from your personal injury claim. When I say they are going to make one payment to you, one time, when you sign a release that is on your personal injury claim. I repeat, it is a critical piece of information, and here's why.

Many times, people are involved in a car accident, and they say the other driver, the bad driver, ran the red light, so I will send them my medical bills, and they will pay them because he ran the red light. Well, that is not the system in Kansas. That's the first piece of critical information you need to know, so there's no sense sending your medical bills or a statement saying you can't work, and your wage loss to the bad driver. Here's what you need to do:

First, you need to get your hands on the automobile accident report, which was completed by the investigating police officer. The reason that this is so important is because the police officer writes down his opinion of who he thinks is at fault in causing the collision. The bad driver's insurance is not going to pay any money; nothing on the property damage, nothing on the personal injury claim until they have a determination that their insured is at fault and caused the accident. They're going to get a copy of the accident report, so you need a copy of the accident report.

Just a minute ago, I mentioned your property damage claim, and that is a claim that usually is resolved within the first thirty days. You notify the bad driver's insurance of where your car is located. They will send an adjuster out and look at the car damage and determine whether the car can be repaired or replaced.

Another option is to contact your insurance company to see if you have what is called collision coverage. You can have your insurance company's adjuster look at the car and determine whether it can be repaired, or whether they are going to total it out and pay you the replacement value. When you contact your own insurance company, usually there is a deductible, which you have to pay. When your insurance company pays for either the repair or the replacement, they will then make a claim against the bad driver's insurance company to get reimbursed the money they paid out.

The second important piece of information you need to know is that your insurance company cannot help you make a claim for what's called "personal/bodily injury"; your medical bills, your wage loss, incurred in the past and those you're expected to incur in the future and your pain and suffering. Your insurance company has their own best self-interest in mind. They want to get back the money they've paid to you or the money they've paid for you.

Next, you also want a copy of the police report in case the adverse insurance wants to take a taped statement from you. So one of the steps you need to take is to give notice of your injury to the adverse insurance company, and usually their next step is to ask … to take a recorded statement from you. You do not want to give them a recorded statement. Give them a copy of the accident report and tell them that is your statement. That's a great strategy to use.

You also need to give notice of your injury to your own insurance company, and here's how the process works in Kansas. Send your medical bills and your wage loss documentation to your own insurance company. They are required under Kansas law to pay you benefits, according to your insurance policy. You paid a premium for these benefits. Usually they'll send you forms which need to be filled out, and you submit these forms, and then they pay benefits.

The next step is that you need to follow up with your medical providers and obtain your bills and obtain documentation for your wage loss. Make sure that you keep all these in one place so that you can get them as necessary. You want to determine if you have health insurance or if you're over sixty-five, Medicare. If you have some type of disability you might be on a state plan such as, Medicaid. If you have these then you're eligible to submit your medical bills to either your health insurance or these government-assisted programs. You do this after your insurance company has finished paying the benefits they are required by law to pay.

Finally, the last piece of information that you need to know, is that for each of these steps, when you begin a claims process, it requires time and effort on your part. It may require multiple telephone calls to follow up on obtaining your medical benefits, or having your health insurance pay your medical bills.

It helps to have a checklist with the dates for when an action is completed. A checklist eliminates worry, anxiety and fear of mistake.

What I developed after thirty-five years of struggling, and talking with ten-thousand people injured in car accident cases, is a two-hundred-and-fifty-two-point checklist. My checklist is computerized. I have a process where, if a checklist item is missed, I'm notified and I can follow up. That checklist helps me eliminate fear, anxiety, and worry so that I can move my cases faster and more efficiently. For you, as a bonus, I enclose a copy of the first checklist I use to help my clients as I advise, guide, and protect them thru the process of obtaining a money recovery for their claims.

TOP 10 CHECKLIST

1. You should have three (3), and possibly four (4), different claim numbers for your car accident:

a. No Fault or Personal Injury Protection (PIP) claim number that you provide to your medical providers;

b. Property damage claim number for auto repairs either through your insurance company if you have collision coverage or through the drivers insurance company;

c. The Liability claim number for the driver's insurance coverage – this may be, and probably is, the same as the property damage claim number;

d. The Uninsured (UM) claim number from *your* insurance company if the bad driver/adverse driver did *not* have insurance.

2. You should be receiving treatment for your injury(s) and should have obtained a doctor's written statement regarding your physical restrictions and/or inability due to injury to perform your job duties – you need to mail this doctor's statement to *your* PIP carrier;

3. You should have received your PIP application, provided the requested information and returned to your PIP carrier;

4. You should have obtained wage verification from your employer and mailed to your PIP carrier;

5. Your property/vehicle damage should be fixed or you have been paid the "fair market value" if your vehicle was *totaled*;

6. You should have obtained the records and bills from the medical providers for EMS, Emergency Room, Emergency Doctor (yes, it's separate from the ER Room bill), surgeons or specialists, radiologists and the hospital (if admitted);

7. Hopefully you have received your first wage loss check – if not contact your PIP carrier;

8. You need to keep a *written* log of the time, expenses, mileage and names of those who help you to do the things you cannot do now that you were able to do for yourself before the injury – such as laundry, cleaning house, grocery shopping, driving to doctors' appointments, etc. – these activities are known as *Essential Services.*

9. You need to send a copy of your Essential Service log to your PIP carrier with a demand for payment at $25 a day. NOTE: You'll also have to submit an updated doctors note stating your limitations each time you send in your log.

10. You need to WATCH THE DATE! Remember that in most cases you only have ***2 years from the date of your accident*** to either settle your claims or file a law suit. Please note that the time limitation date is different for minors and uninsured/underinsured cases.

If you would like help with your car accident injury case,
first review the copy below of the
100% Satisfaction Guarantee.

If that meets with your approval then call toll-fee
1-866-303-1411
to schedule an office appointment
or a telephone conference with Mr. Hogan.

The Law Center for Car Accident Injuries

SAMPLE

Dan -

My Personal Promise to *You*

As a valued client I want you **100% SATISFIED** with your decision to hire me as your lawyer.

You should know within **90 DAYS** whether or not I am the ***right*** lawyer for you.

So, I offer you a

RISK-FREE PROMISE, NO QUESTIONS ASKED

GUARANTEE!

If you are **NOT 100% SATISFIED** with my services you can fire me and

NOT OWE ME 1 PENNY!

CALL TOLL-FREE

1-866-303-1411

SATISFACTION 100% GUARANTEE

Paul Hogan, Attorney
Licensed in Kansas and Oklahoma

NOTES

1
WHY YOU HAVE A CASE AND THE OTHER DRIVER IS TO BLAME

It's Friday night, I am leaving the drive-thru restaurant with dinner for my family. It is sleeting and the streets are slushy. I'm on a four lane street, driving in the center lane, when an oncoming pickup crosses the center line. I'm thinking, "Oh! No, don't do this!" He is heading right for me. I think he's making a left turn. I stand on my brakes and slammed the steering wheel to the right hoping I miss him. Somehow in the middle of this maneuver, he has now turned back and I T-bone him right behind the driver's door. There is this sound, the loud crash, an explosion, and the sound of metal tearing. The steering will spins out of my control. I feel the seatbelt harness jerk me. Smoke fills the cabin of my pickup. I can't breathe. My mind is racing. I'm on fire! I've got to get out of here now! I fumble and unhook the seatbelt harness and get out into the cold winter air.

Later, I realize my truck was not on fire. My airbag exploded, protecting me, doing exactly what it was designed to do. I don't know whether I checked the other driver or he checked me, but I'm mad at him for being stupid. It turns out he was not turning left at the intersection, but that is where he lost control because he was driving too fast for slushy roads. I'm really mad. The front end of my pickup truck is smashed back into the engine compartment and past the front wheel. It's for sure not drivable. I'm thinking, "Is this guy going to fess up and tell the truth to the police when they get here? Are they going to give him a ticket?"

What a hassle! Then, all of a sudden, my shoulders jerk upwards towards my ears. My back and neck muscles tighten. I foresee doctor's visits, and probably physical therapy in my near future. I hope this guy has insurance. How much time is this going to take out of my life? What am I going to have to do to get a rental? I really am mad at this jerk for upsetting my life. Doctor's visits, physical therapy, rental cars, dealing with multiple telephone calls to insurance adjusters- hassle, hassle, hassle. I am a car accident lawyer. This happens to my clients, not to me. I really wish this guy would have paid attention. I didn't do anything wrong. I tried to avoid this collision. How is his insurance company going to try to twist this? Are they going to say I was going too fast for the slushy streets? There are no skid marks. Will they say I was not paying attention?

Losing control and crossing the center line is a driving error. Running a stop sign, failure to yield the right-of-way, turning left into oncoming traffic, running into the rear of a vehicle stopped in traffic are also all examples of driving errors. Most injury accidents are caused by driving errors. So if you are injured as the result of someone committing a driving error, then that someone is at fault and you have a case. Legally, you can make a claim. A driver has a duty to maintain control of their vehicle, for example; to stop at a red light, to yield the right of way to oncoming traffic when making a left hand turn and to avoid colliding with a vehicle stopped in traffic in front of them. I had a case, I made a claim, and I made a recovery. The basis of a legal claim is a duty and a breach of the duty which causes damages or injury.

So, do you have a case?

Common sense tells you whether or not you have a case. As a general rule, laws are based upon common sense. In other words, if you can figure out what is the difference between a right action and a wrong action, the law usually supports the right action. This is not rocket science. You do not need a Harvard Law professor to tell you that you have a case because a bad driver ran a red light, rear ended you while you were stopped, or any other failure to obey traffic laws which resulted in a collision.

Again, the basis for making a legal claim is a simple, three step analysis. First, there must be a duty. It is the duty of every driver to obey traffic laws. Second, there must be a breach of the duty, such as when a driver violates the traffic laws, that driver breaches the duty to obey traffic laws. Third, there must be causation; the breach of the duty causes the car accident and the resulting injury.

Once you have determined the other driver is at fault, you then assess/analyze the injury. Imagine if you were driving down the street, on your way to the grocery store, in your lane of traffic, obeying all traffic laws, and the car in the lane next to you abruptly swerved and glanced off your bumper, leaving a scratch on your bumper, and you tore a fake fingernail from your little pinky finger. According to our above analysis, you would have a case. Is it worth pursuing? Certainly, to get the scratch repaired. But, would you spend a year of your time to risk thousands of dollars to pursue a personal injury claim for your fake fingernail? Probably not.

On the other hand, same fact situation; you are on the way to the grocery store when the car next to you swerves into you, forcing you to jump the curb, hitting a tree, breaking your arm, resulting in extensive medical treatment and your inability to work for a long period of time. Is this worth pursuing? Yes.

If you would like help with your car accident injury case,
first review the copy below of the
100% Satisfaction Guarantee.

If that meets with your approval then call toll-fee
1-866-303-1411
to schedule an office appointment
or a telephone conference with Mr. Hogan.

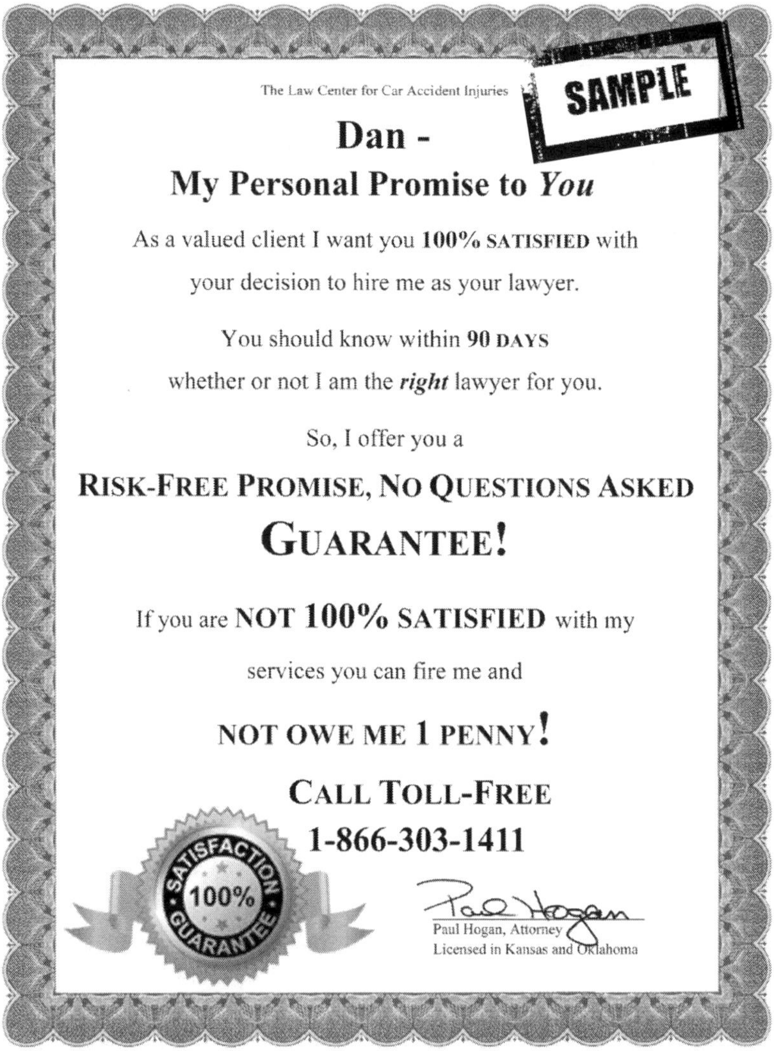

The Law Center for Car Accident Injuries

SAMPLE

Dan -

My Personal Promise to *You*

As a valued client I want you **100% SATISFIED** with your decision to hire me as your lawyer.

You should know within **90 DAYS** whether or not I am the ***right*** lawyer for you.

So, I offer you a

RISK-FREE PROMISE, NO QUESTIONS ASKED

GUARANTEE!

If you are **NOT 100% SATISFIED** with my services you can fire me and

NOT OWE ME 1 PENNY!

CALL TOLL-FREE
1-866-303-1411

SATISFACTION 100% GUARANTEE

Paul Hogan, Attorney
Licensed in Kansas and Oklahoma

NOTES

2
IMPORTANT NEWS HOW TO GET YOUR CAR FIXED/REPLACED

Guys all remember their first car, the hours spent washing, waxing and polishing their baby. Country songs are written about the first car. Women name their cars, usually a feminine name like Suzie or Rosie.

Here is my experience. I come to the hospital. I see a young man who has fractured bones with rods holding them in place, tubes all over the place. I asked him "what is your biggest concern?" Yeah, you know the answer. Through the pain a tortured voice asked, "What about my car?" Here are the answers to questions regarding property damage.

Janie was in my office last week after being injured in a car accident. Besides her injury, her concern was her beloved pickup. She explained it was paid for, well maintained. She recently bought new tires and paid for some minor mechanical repairs. In her words, it was good, reliable transportation. She needed a car to get to the doctor.

Here are the issues Janie faced that you could face. First, there has to be some insurance coverage. One of two things must occur. One option is that the bad driver's insurance accepts liability after a determination is made that their driver is at fault. Usually there is a delay of days or sometimes weeks or more before they "step up to bat" and deal with your loss of transportation.

The other option is to make a claim on your insurance if you have collision coverage including a rental rider, which provides a rental car while your car is being repaired. Usually when making a claim on your own insurance policy, there is a deductible involved. Both options take time. If you have collision coverage with a rental rider, by all means use this service you paid for. If not, and you have the wherewithal, cash/money, a credit card, or someone that will loan you money, then go rent a car. Many car rental companies have policies and procedures which can make this a challenge, such as only renting to those who are 25; only renting to one whose name is on the credit card, etc. But renting your own car is the fastest, easiest way and you will get reimbursed.

Janie did not have the money to rent a car or a credit card with available credit. I explained to her that until they decide whether they want to repair or replace (and by replace I mean pay her the fair market value of her truck) then Janie could make a claim for her loss of use of her car, for each day until the insurance decided which option they chose. So, if they do decide to repair, they will offer a rental car during the repair time.

A frequently asked question is "Do I have to take it to their shop?" The answer is no. We live in America; we have the freedom to choose. However, many insurance companies offer a lifetime guarantee on the repairs if you use their

preferred provider. But again, so do many auto repair shops. The point is who will be in business when you need them – the local shop or the insurance company. As I stated earlier, the law requires the insurance company to do one of two things – either repair or replace your damaged car.
Because they pay one way or the other, they get to choose. You cannot force them to spend $5,000.00 or $10,000.00 to repair a $2,000.00 car because your favorite uncle gave it to you. If they choose not to repair your car because the repair costs are close to equal or exceed the value of the car, then they must pay you the "fair market value" of your vehicle.

Think of that concept in another way:. If you sold your car on the open market the day before the accident, what would it bring in its condition? Age, mileage, hail dents and interior appearance are all factors. There are some sources to help determine a range of value such as a local car dealer maybe where you purchased the car. They would love to help you so they can sell you another car. The Internet has many sites for example Google, eBay or kellybluebook.com. In a local newspaper you can search and see what dealers and private sellers are listing prices at. The NADA, "National Association of Dealers," has a compilation of area used car prices.

So what happened to Janie? Initially the adverse insurance company instructed her to go to Enterprise and rent a car. Enterprise said the insurance company did not give them authorization and that Janie needed $200.00 cash to rent a vehicle or have $200.00 available credit on her credit card. Janie did not have either and she left without a rental car for the weekend. On the following Monday, an adjuster examined Janie's pickup. He determined it was a total loss. He provided a rental car for her until she received her check for the value of her pickup and the loss of use.

To summarize, *ultimately* your car will be fixed or you will receive money to replace it. An important point to remember is during the period you are without a car; you have a claim for loss of use, basically the cost of a comparable daily rental car. You now know what to expect in dealing with your property damage claim.

If you would like help with your car accident injury case,
first review the copy below of the
100% Satisfaction Guarantee.

If that meets with your approval then call toll-fee
1-866-303-1411
to schedule an office appointment
or a telephone conference with Mr. Hogan.

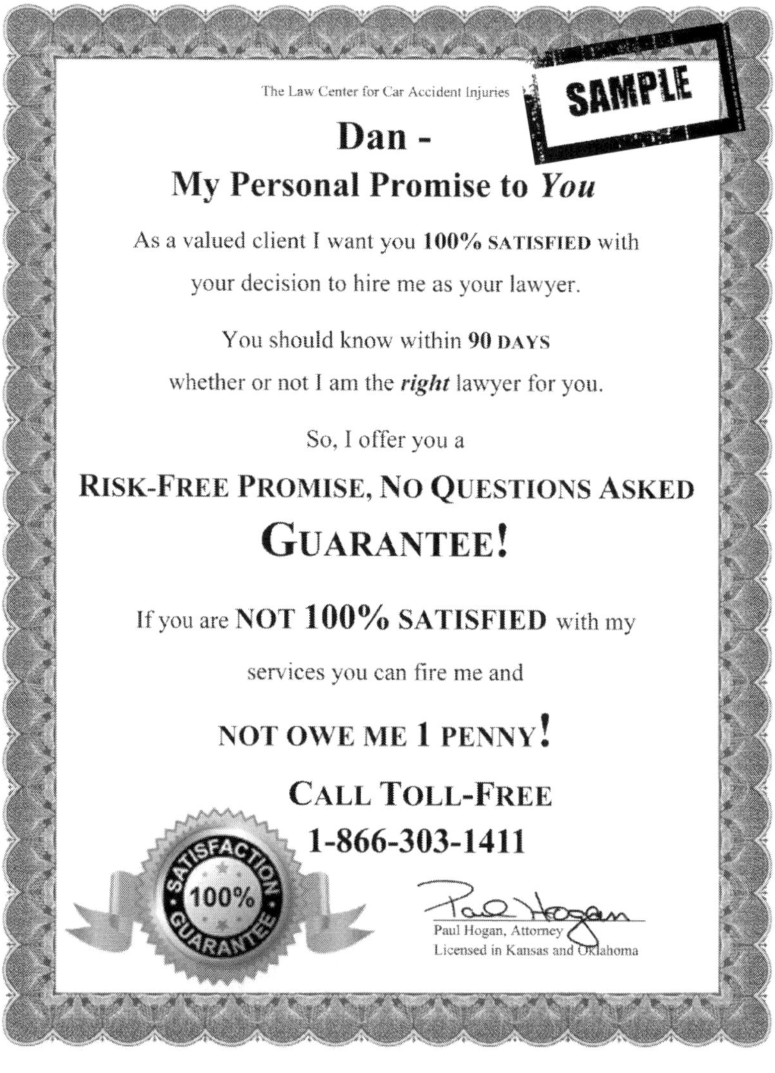

The Law Center for Car Accident Injuries

SAMPLE

Dan -

My Personal Promise to *You*

As a valued client I want you **100% SATISFIED** with your decision to hire me as your lawyer.

You should know within **90 DAYS** whether or not I am the ***right*** lawyer for you.

So, I offer you a

RISK-FREE PROMISE, NO QUESTIONS ASKED GUARANTEE!

If you are **NOT 100% SATISFIED** with my services you can fire me and

NOT OWE ME 1 PENNY!

CALL TOLL-FREE
1-866-303-1411

Paul Hogan, Attorney
Licensed in Kansas and Oklahoma

NOTES

3
WHAT YOU CAN DO TO PAY YOUR MEDICAL BILLS

When the topic is about money, or the lack of money, especially when bills are due, this can be an emotional issue. It's like when my dad went bankrupt in the oil business with five kids to feed, ages three to eighteen. My memory is my parents fighting, fighting a lot, always about money or rather *no* money.

I want you to know, that if I could, I would waive a magic wand and make this all go away or I would write you a check for whatever amount is needed to help you and your family.

The rules which allow me to practice law prohibit me from making loans to my clients. To do so would be an ethical violation, and I could lose my license to practice law.

Here are rules of the road as we journey towards the destination of making a money recovery.

The most important point to keep in mind is on your bodily injury claim, the bad drivers insurance is going to make one payment to you one time. This occurs when you sign a release saying you are not going to come back and make a claim for one penny more. You do not want to do this when you are in the midst of medical treatment, not knowing the extent of treatment and the final amount of those bills.

Do not look to the bad driver's insurance to help you. **They don't care!**

Disclaimer: This does not pertain to your property damage, for now, it is a separate claim. It is usually resolved within the first 30 days without attorney involvement.

WHAT DO YOU DO? HOW DO YOU FIND HELP?
WHERE DO YOU LOOK?

First, examine your insurance policy to determine if there are medical and wage loss benefits available to you. If so, make a claim for those benefits.

Possibly you have employment benefits, such as health insurance and/or possible both short-term and long-term disability benefits.

Other resources may include seeking a loan from a bank or credit union, possibly family or friends can help.

A last resort, one which I advise against and do not recommend, is applying for a loan on your settlement. These loans carry high fees and high interest rates. I recognize when it comes to feeding your children, making a mortgage or rental payment, you may not have another option. What is important is you need to understand the risks and disadvantages.

Although this can be challenging and a difficult time, it will pass, it is temporary. This is information you need to survive while you undergo medical treatment and while your claim is pending. What I have learned from my friends injured is a long as there is an insurance policy; there is a money fund t make a claim for your medical bills, your wage loss, and any other losses. You should expect to make a money recovery.

Red Flag Warning! Even if the bad driver's insurance adjuster states they want to pay you their policy limits because of your "major injury" STOP! There are two issues to be aware of which could cost you thousands, or tens of thousands, of dollars.

1. If you accept a liability settlement you may lose your future personal injury protection benefits such as wage loss, rehabilitation, or essential services.
2. If you accept a liability settlement you may lose tens of thousands of dollars more in Underinsured Motorist benefits unless you follow a very specific legal procedure to preserve your claim.

K.S.A. 40-284(f) states:

An underinsured motorist coverage insurer shall have subrogation rights under the provisions of K.S.A. 40-287 and amendments thereto. If a tentative agreement to settle for liability limits has been reached with the underinsured tortfeasor, written notice must be given by certified mail to the underinsured motorist coverage insurer by its insured. Such written notice shall include written authorization or a court order to obtain reports from all employers and medical providers. Within 60 days of receipt of this written notice, the underinsured motorist coverage insurer may substitute payment to the insured for the tentative settlement amount. The underinsured motorist coverage insurer is then subrogated to the extent of such payment and any settlement under the underinsured motorist coverage. If the underinsured motorist coverage insurer fails to pay the insured the amount of the tentative settlement within 60 days, the underinsured motorist coverage insurer has no right of subrogation for any amount paid under the underinsured motorist coverage.

NOTES

If you would like help with your car accident injury case,

first review the copy below of the
100% Satisfaction Guarantee.

If that meets with your approval then call toll-fee
1-866-303-1411
to schedule an office appointment
or a telephone conference with Mr. Hogan.

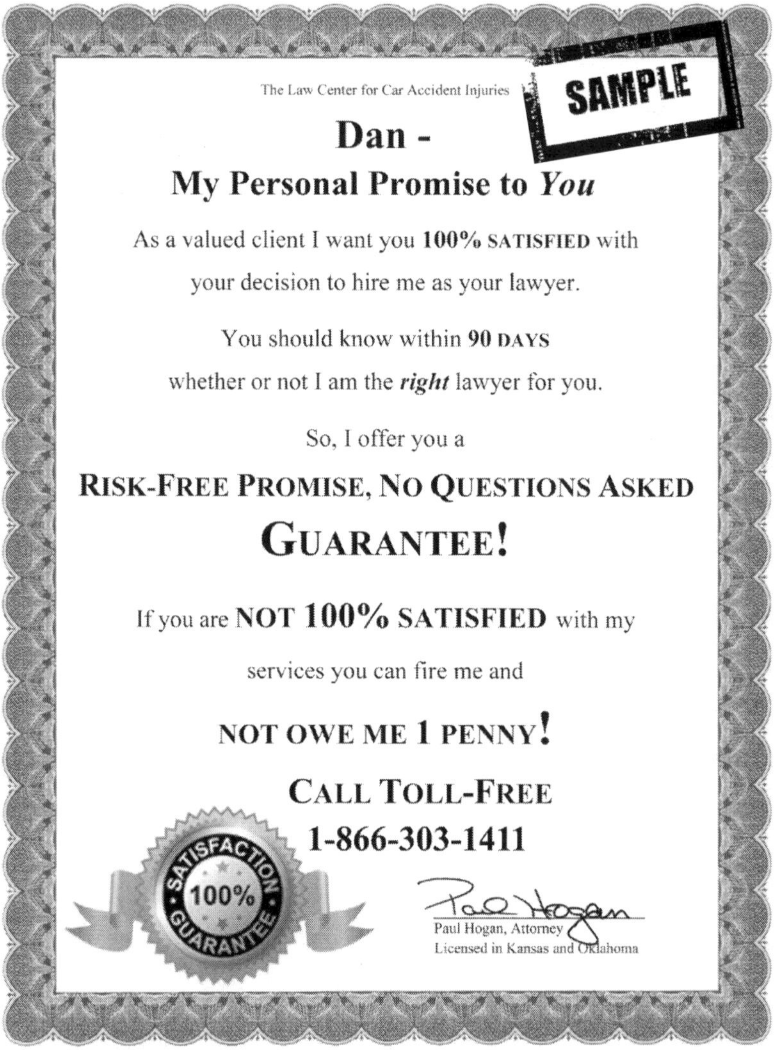

The Law Center for Car Accident Injuries

SAMPLE

Dan -

My Personal Promise to *You*

As a valued client I want you **100% SATISFIED** with
your decision to hire me as your lawyer.

You should know within **90 DAYS**
whether or not I am the ***right*** lawyer for you.

So, I offer you a

RISK-FREE PROMISE, NO QUESTIONS ASKED

GUARANTEE!

If you are **NOT 100% SATISFIED** with my
services you can fire me and

NOT OWE ME 1 PENNY!

CALL TOLL-FREE
1-866-303-1411

SATISFACTION 100% GUARANTEE

Paul Hogan, Attorney
Licensed in Kansas and Oklahoma

4
THE STEP YOU NEED TO TAKE TO MAKE A CLAIM FOR FUTURE MEDICAL TREATMENT AND ONGOING ISSUES

What happens as time goes by and you have reached a plateau in your medical treatment? Your doctor says you have to "learn to live with it." You are told there is no medical treatment that will cure you, or, you are not a candidate for surgery. How do you present a claim for future medical treatment?

Again, documentation is the rule. You must obtain from your doctor the specialized medical records which contain the diagnosis. For example, if you suffer pain from damaged disks and you have diabetes (which increases the risk of failing to obtain a meaningful recovery) your orthopedic doctor might say, you could go through an invasive complex two disk laminectomy surgery with fixation (which involves removing of part of the bony structure of the neck and implanting rods and plates) to stabilize your neck. His opinion is that, with the operation, you have a 50/50 shot of becoming pain free. With that opinion, you may choose not to have surgery.

In order to present a claim you need not only the doctor's opinion in writing but in addition, a medical professional's opinion that the neck injury was caused by a car accident. At the *very* least, a diagnosis that states your neck condition was aggravated by the car accident. You also need the doctor's opinion of any future medical treatment necessary, such as pain medication, a yearly MRI or diagnostic tests to monitor your conditions. Finally, you'll need an estimate of the yearly cost of the medical treatment, the inflation rate of medical treatment costs, and document your life expectancy.

Many times the treating doctors are not capable of providing the required information other than the condition, the surgical option, and the risk. Most physicians are far removed from knowledge of the cost of medical treatment. In that case it may be necessary to hire a specialist to provide a report, such as physiatrists, who are doctors specializing in rehabilitation medicine.

Often times, a person may choose not to undergo a surgical process at this time, even if the doctor believes it will help and there is only small risk. The decision may be that they want the insurance company to pay them for future surgery. After going to the time and expense of documenting this type of claim, many insurance companies simply balk and may refuse to evaluate or pay for future medical claims. Their adjustors cite "experience" that they had paid for surgery and the claimant would then keep the money and not have the surgery. Thus, they do not voluntarily pay such claims.

The good news is that the law recognizes future medical expense claims. The bad news is because it is so commonplace for insurance adjusters to refuse to evaluate or pay these claims that if you want money for this, you will probably need an attorney and should be prepared to go through the litigation process.

Remember that in almost all cases, we are dealing with claims against insurance policies. As stated at the end of Chapter 1. Insurance policies have limits, meaning the total amount that the insurance company is responsible to pay for is based upon the premium the customer paid for the policy. For example: In Kansas for personal injury, the minimum liability policy limits required by law are $25,000 per person limit and, a $50,000 per collision limit. This is referred to as split limits coverage. This means the maximum an insurance company would pay to any one person injured in a car accident is $25,000. If there was more than one person injured, for example, three people were injured and each of their claims were valued at $25,000, the insurance company would not pay $75,000 ($25,000 to each person) but would pay their limits of $50,000, which in most cases would be divided equally. A total of $16,333.

Insurance policies are usually issued in step ups, beginning at 25/50, then 50/100, or 100 /300 with each limit as explained above. At the $300,000 level. The policy may be single limit coverage, meaning any one injured person or any number of injured persons can claim up to the $300,000 limit. Some policies may be a 300/500 policy. Again, any one person would be subject to the $300,000 limit and all injured persons, no matter the number would be limited to $500,000 limit.

Most car accidents are between two individuals. There are collisions between an individual and a commercial vehicle. Commercial vehicles usually carry high policy limits.

The important thing to consider, when making a claim for future medical expenses, is that you may have a claim where the value of your injury when only considering the existing medical expenses (without extra consideration for the future medical expense) the value of your case may exceed the policy limits as explained above. As an example, if you have a fractured bone and $15,000 in medical expenses and your bad driver's policy only has a $25,000 per person limit for the liability claim; then you probably would not need to go through the time and expense of documenting any claim for future medical treatment or expenses.

The types of injuries that can be the basis for future medical expense claims are usually injuries to the joints – the wrist, elbow, shoulder, ankle, knee, hip and spine. Also any type of traumatic brain injury. It is important to note, in order to make a claim for future medical, a doctor has to state that the future medical treatment is probable, meaning more likely true than not true (as compared to a doctor saying it is possible, a possibility can be defined as a 1% chance of something happening, and usually a possibility is not admissible as evidence). Also, he has to state the medical treatment is needed due to the accident and give an estimate of the cost.

At this point, let me take my lawyer hat off, so to speak and put on my father's hat. I give you my life's experiences, my loving advice, as I would to a family member. This advice has nothing to do with legalities.

Thinking of the future when recovering from an injury can drive one crazy with fear, doubt, and anxiety. No one knows what the future will bring. Many who worry about the future choose to use faith and prayer. When dealing with the future my parental, fatherly advice is based on the good book, as I refer to the Bible, I also refer to principles advocated in the Alcoholics Anonymous program.

The only time any of us is given is this 24 hours to do what we can with our existence on God's good earth. Worrying about tomorrow, next week, next month and next year is a waste of time, thought and energy. God forbid, but it could happen and we hear about all the time. What a waste of time worrying if you died in your sleep tonight? The point being, take whatever action you need to take today. Rest and quit worrying. Be more active, if need be after a time of inactivity.

The point is, focus on what action you can take today. As our grandparents said, "Quit worrying about the future, tomorrow will bring its own set of problems." When my clients call me with an anxious tone questioning their future, questioning what if; I let them talk, ventilate, get it out of their system. I then ask if I can take off my lawyer hat and put on my father's hat and I give the above described advice. Further, when I am asked questions about how to handle life issues while their claim is pending; my answer is always the same -- make the decision that is best for your life, *now*. Think in terms that there is no case pending (for whatever reason). Then make your decision. Finally, I suggest living one day at a time. And when in doubt, say a prayer;

God grant me the serenity to accept the things I cannot change. The courage to change the things that I can, and the wisdom to know the difference.

NOTES

If you would like help with your car accident injury case,
first review the copy below of the
100% Satisfaction Guarantee.

If that meets with your approval then call toll-fee
1-866-303-1411
to schedule an office appointment
or a telephone conference with Mr. Hogan.

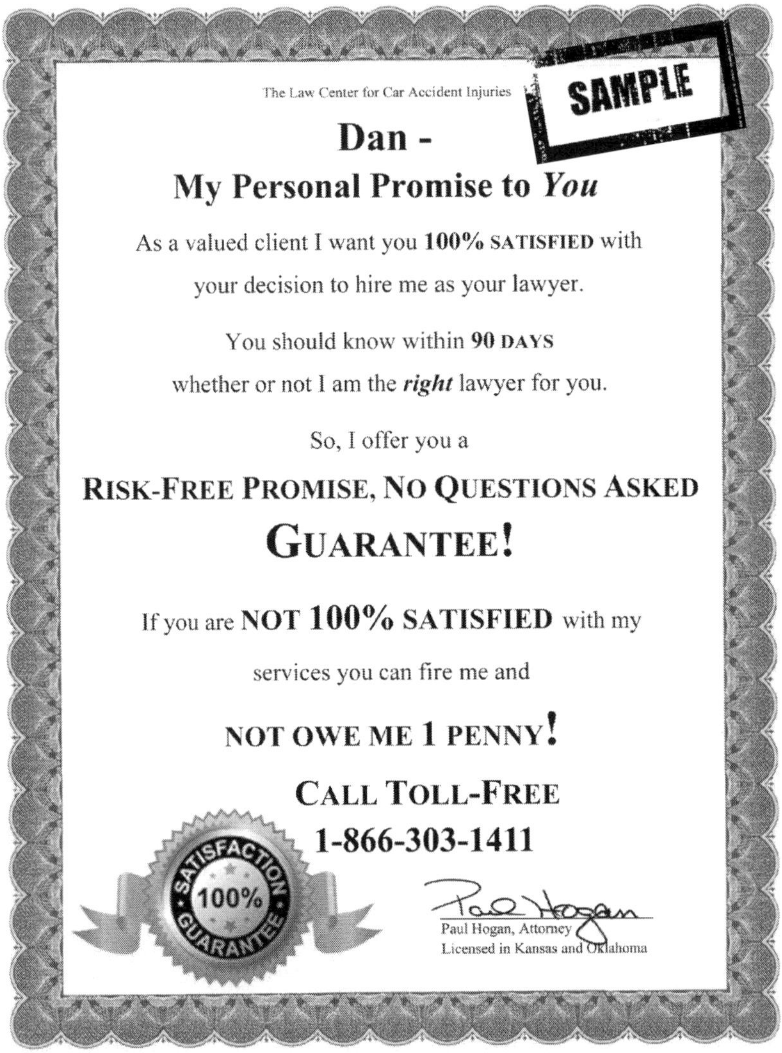

SAMPLE

The Law Center for Car Accident Injuries

Dan -

My Personal Promise to *You*

As a valued client I want you **100% SATISFIED** with
your decision to hire me as your lawyer.

You should know within **90 DAYS**
whether or not I am the ***right*** lawyer for you.

So, I offer you a

RISK-FREE PROMISE, NO QUESTIONS ASKED

GUARANTEE!

If you are **NOT 100% SATISFIED** with my
services you can fire me and

NOT OWE ME 1 PENNY!

CALL TOLL-FREE
1-866-303-1411

Paul Hogan, Attorney
Licensed in Kansas and Oklahoma

5
WHAT TO DO NEXT WHEN YOUR DOCTOR RELEASES YOU FROM TREATMENT

Documentation is critical. Paper equals dollars. You should begin your settlement demand with why you should make a recovery. The initial focus is not on you, but the driving error of the bad driver which caused the accident.

In chapter 1 we discussed the basis of why you have a claim. Now ignore all that information and focus with a laser beam on that one driving error that caused the accident. Usually the investigating police officer summarizes the driving error in the official accident report in what I call "police speak." For example: Vehicle One failed to stop at a stop sign. Your translation would be something like, "Jones, utterly disregarded stopping at the stop sign colliding with Smith. As a result, Smith was injured and transported to XYZ hospital.

Next is a written summary of medical treatment, beginning with the initial examination tests and a diagnosis by the emergency room doctor. Continue on describing any treatment, prescriptions and doctor's order for additional medical care. Also include the doctor's order for taking off work, if applicable.

Note that documentation and description is a detail oriented task. It is the most arduous and challenging task to be done.

Continue onward, detailing any hospitalization, each doctor's visit, noting the complaints listed in the records, the diagnosis, the doctors' opinions, and any specialist opinions. Keep track of all the treatment, all dates of diagnostic testing such as MRIs, x-rays etc. and the dates of physical therapy, including any dates missed and an explanation such as lack of transportation or flu occurring.

Note: Adjuster's like to count the numbers of physical therapy visits and the number of missed appointments. So it's better to point this out initially.

After you've finished the recitation of medical treatment in chronological order, then list with specificity, each medical provider and their total medical bills charged.

Next, detail the wage loss by noting that on (dd/mo/yr) Dr. Jones issued a written work restriction and the date you were released to return to work. Sometimes there are multiple doctors issuing restrictions and all must be listed. List your employer, your job description and why the injury kept you from working. Write down your usual hours per week and your rate of pay -- hourly or salary, with the total amount of wage loss. Also note, if you cannot return to work, the projected amount of future wage loss.

Keep in mind that if you are dealing with a permanent injury and a permanent inability to work, use an actuarial table with your life expectancy and compute your projected wage loss to retirement at age 65. Add a figure for part time from 65 to whatever age your life details are justified.

Continue by listing all of your medical expenses -- past and future, wage loss, past and future, and any incidental expenses or other losses. These may include your pharmacy bills, mileage, etc.

Now, list your essential services. List the total hours that someone helped you do the things you normally would've done for yourself but for the injury. List the total hours, times and the current market value rate. Call a home care company and ask their hourly rate, usually it falls between $15 and $20 an hour depending on the locale.

By now you have a list that looks similar to this:

Total medical expense incurred to date

$______________________________

Total wage loss incurred to date

$______________________________

Future wage loss

$______________________________

Future Medical Expense

$______________________________

Other expenses and losses

$______________________________

Essential Services

$______________________________

Mileage

$______________________________

Subtotal:

$______________________________

Here is a formula for making a demand. Please note, this is not the only formula and there is no definitive standard formula for making a demand. You should take into consideration the injury, whether or not there were fractures or surgeries, and whether or not it is permanent injury that will affect your life activities for your life span. The more serious the injury and its effects are, then the higher the demand.

Reality is insurance companies do not consider paying the initial demand. And if they do, <u>then you made a big mistake by not demanding enough</u>. So the formula for making a demand is for at least 10 times your medical expense, as a figure for your *<u>pain and suffering</u>*. Please note that most, if not all, insurance companies are not going to voluntarily pay 10 times the medical expenses as a figure for pain and suffering, especially upon the initial demand. Then add all your losses, and you have a figure to use to begin the next process - negotiating. Remember, this is an initial demand, and we are dealing with insurance policies. You will *always* add to your demand number the language **"or policy limits, whichever is greater."**

Pain and suffering

$___________________________

Total:

$___________________________

If you would like help with your car accident injury case,
first review the copy below of the
100% Satisfaction Guarantee.

If that meets with your approval then call toll-fee
1-866-303-1411
to schedule an office appointment
or a telephone conference with Mr. Hogan.

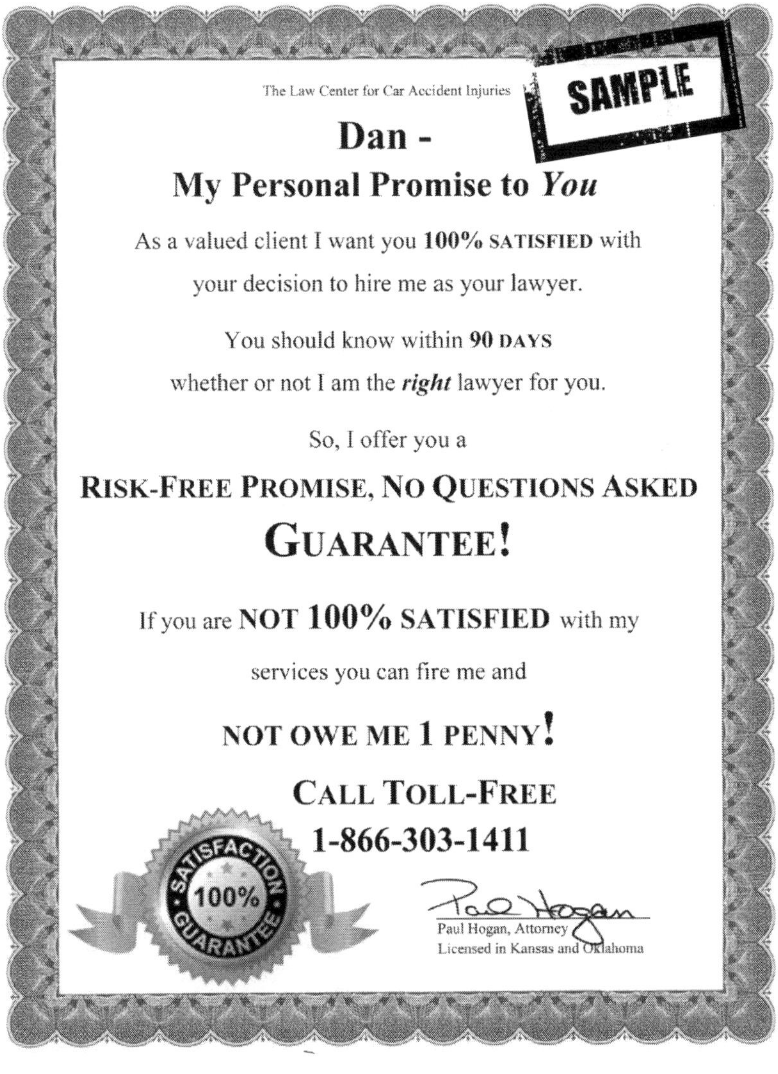

SAMPLE

The Law Center for Car Accident Injuries

Dan -

My Personal Promise to *You*

As a valued client I want you **100% SATISFIED** with your decision to hire me as your lawyer.

You should know within **90 DAYS** whether or not I am the ***right*** lawyer for you.

So, I offer you a

RISK-FREE PROMISE, NO QUESTIONS ASKED

GUARANTEE!

If you are **NOT 100% SATISFIED** with my services you can fire me and

NOT OWE ME 1 PENNY!

CALL TOLL-FREE

1-866-303-1411

SATISFACTION 100% GUARANTEE

Paul Hogan, Attorney
Licensed in Kansas and Oklahoma

NOTES

6
WHEN DO YOU GET THE MONEY YOU DESERVE?

The quick answer is you get your settlement money when you sign a release stating you will not make any further claims. Remember, you only get paid one time after you sign a release. So the best advice I can give you is that, you should UNDER NO CIRCUMSTANCES sign a release during ongoing medical treatment without first seeking legal advice.

The more accurate answer, at least in my office is that our average case length is 9 months from the date we open a case to the date we close the case. Notice that I highlight "average" case length and that there are a multitude of factors that influence the time to settlement. Some of these factors are the facts of the case such as; are there fault issues? What type of injury is it? What is the length of treatment? Was full health recovered or are there ongoing health issues? Is there enough insurance money available to compensate for all issues? Is that specific insurance carrier willing to negotiate timely and reach a settlement? Does the client want to settle and give authority to reach a very specific settlement amount or does this case need to proceed to the litigation process which involves more time, expense and risk? Is there an underinsured claim that needs specific legal action before you settle the liability claim? When placed in this situation as I pointed out in the Disclaimer at the beginning of the book, laws can change by courts and legislative bodies. The procedure for making an Uninsured Motorist Claim and giving notice when attempting a settlement is set forth at KSA 40-284(f). Also, KSA 40-284€(5) requires notice to the underinsured insurance company when suit is filed against the uninsured motorist.

Here are 2 examples of settlement time frames –

Carl Client suffers a fractured leg, incurs $35,000 in medical bills, a wage loss of $10,000 and is on crutches for 12 weeks. His case is valued by his lawyer at more than $100,000. The bad driver causing the wreck has an insurance policy with limits up to $25,000, which they offer to Carl. The bad driver has no other assets with which to pay Carl. Carl has no insurance policies applicable that will pay him additional money. This is the type of case where you accept the limits offered, you settle the case quickly, basically taking the money and run, as there is no reason to keep the liability case open (unless you are receiving PIP benefits). You may have other issue such as dealing with medical bills, hospital liens, personal injury protection liens; again the liability claim is settled.

Other times a case may take longer, involving the same facts with the exception that Carl has an insurance policy with limits up to $300,000 that pays him for his damages. Kansas law requires/mandates a specific procedure to be followed in order to make the underinsured claim. Failure to do so forfeits your rights to make an underinsured claim and may cost you tens or hundreds of thousands of dollars. I emphasize seeking a lawyer's help when placed in this situation. Also, in this case, you would wait for Carl to finish all medical treatment. Then, obtain a doctor's opinion about his needs for future medical treatment and the cost as Carl ages. After obtaining documentation, negotiation begins to obtain the maximum amount. If an agreement cannot be reached through negotiation then litigation is usually the last option. As you can see all this takes effort and time.

I am no different than most, and when I was injured in a car accident I wanted the most money I could get as fast as possible with the least amount of frustration and hassle.

NOTES

If you would like help with your car accident injury case,
first review the copy below of the
100% Satisfaction Guarantee.

If that meets with your approval then call toll-fee
1-866-303-1411
to schedule an office appointment
or a telephone conference with Mr. Hogan.

The Law Center for Car Accident Injuries

SAMPLE

Dan -

My Personal Promise to *You*

As a valued client I want you **100% SATISFIED** with
your decision to hire me as your lawyer.

You should know within **90 DAYS**
whether or not I am the ***right*** lawyer for you.

So, I offer you a

RISK-FREE PROMISE, NO QUESTIONS ASKED

GUARANTEE!

If you are **NOT 100% SATISFIED** with my
services you can fire me and

NOT OWE ME 1 PENNY!

CALL TOLL-FREE
1-866-303-1411

SATISFACTION 100% GUARANTEE

Paul Hogan, Attorney
Licensed in Kansas and Oklahoma

7
WHAT YOU NEED TO KNOW AND THEY HAVEN'T TOLD YOU ABOUT YOUR MONEY

There are always other issues that arise in the context of a injury car accident. Most are anticipated and usually all injury claims follow a sequence or a pattern. And as we've discussed, it goes something like this: there is first a determination of fault, a confirmation of insurance coverage, and adjustment of the property loss, payment for the repair or replacement value of the auto damaged, medical treatment and a period of recovery from physical injury, a search for insurance to pay for medical bills and wage loss as they are incurred, documentation to prove the valuation of your personal injury, a demand, a response, negotiation to settle a claim, followed by more documentation, and payment of settlement funds.

When you have suffered a "bad" injury and are eligible to make an underinsured motorist claim there is an additional period of time required to give notice as set forth earlier on Page 32. Usually that is a 60 day period but sometimes the underinsured carrier will give permission to accept the offer, waiving the 60 day time period. A better practice is to obtain the permission in <u>writing</u>.

Other issues that can arise and complicate the above sequence are:

1. Were you on the job at the time you were injured in your car accident? If so, you have both a worker's compensation claim and your personal injury claim. This usually adds time as the need arises to determine and settle both legal issues. Unfortunately, because you have two legal issues it does not necessarily mean that it will add money to the valuation of your personal injury. Keep your fingers crossed, it might.

2. If you are eligible for government assistance such as Medicaid the state-level program, Medicare, or Social Security on the federal level, the fact that you are eligible means another layer of time and effort to determine if they paid benefits and the amount that must be reimbursed, if any.

3. If you received health-insurance benefits and that policy and/or the law under which you receive those benefits allows reimbursement. Again, it adds a layer of time and effort to determine the amount of benefits paid and the amount that must be reimbursed.

4. There are liens allowed by law (which means it is lawful and mandatory that the lien amount be withheld from your settlement). Examples of these are unpaid child support, personal injury protection

subrogation liens, and the above described Medicare/Medicaid, sometimes referred to as super liens, because if an attorney or entity like an insurance company fails to make arrangements to honor the lien they can be held liable for the payment of that lien.

5. When dealing with a bad injury you want to make sure you have a very clear understanding of every action by anyone who caused or contributed to your accident. Here is an example: Bob Badly Injured was a passenger in his friend Sam Speeder's car when Victor Violator ran a stop sign colliding with Sam Speeder. Bob suffers a broken leg requiring surgery. He incurs $100,000 in medical expenses and $50,000 in wage loss and now walks with a permanent limp. Victor's insurance has to pay $25,000 policy limits because he ran the stop sign. Bob has no insurance. Bob should look at Sam Speeder's liability insurance as Sam's speed contributed to the resulting collision. The point is that if Sam wasn't speeding the collision might have been avoided or the impact may have been less severe. In such a case you could make a claim against Sam for say 25% of the value of the injury as Victor was 75% at fault for running a stop sign and Sam is 25% at fault for speeding. If Bob's injury is valued at $200,000 x 25% = $50,000 and hopefully Sam has a $50,000 insurance policy.

6. In summary, there can be one or two or more or maybe all the examples affecting your case. It seems like everyone has their hand in your settlement money.

Do I need a lawyer or can I do this myself? The answer is yes, you can do this yourself if you want to take the time, deal with the frustration, worry and fear of making a mistake that ends up costing you money or delays your settlement. First, you have to be prepared to pay money to obtain reports and records. Further, you should keep in mind the following statistics provided by the insurance companies themselves.

53% of Claimants without attorneys receive only 21% of settlement dollars.

Now, you know why insurance companies want you to represent yourself. As a matter of fact, insurance companies **divide cases** into those who are **not attorney represented** and those **who have attorney representation.**

In other words, the **47% of claimants who were represented by attorneys received 79% of all liability payments** (according to the Insurance Research Council's reports in 2003 and 2008).

The Allstate Unrepresented Adjustor Training Manual, dated July 1995 states,

> ". . . represented claims **[when an injured person uses an attorney] settle for 2 to 3 times more** than unrepresented claims [when a person deals directly with the insurer]."

The training manual included the following statistic:

> With settlements under $15,000.00, injured claimants **represented by an attorney** averaged **$7,450.00 in total settlement.**

Those who **represented themselves** to Allstate **averaged $3,464.00 in total settlement.** Doing the math, **retaining an attorney** for a small claim on average **more than doubled (a 115% increase) the likelihood of a better settlement.**

It's NO WONDER insurance adjustors don't want you to seek the advice of an attorney!

Finally, in closing, you only live one day at a time, it is wise to make plans for the future, but it is unwise to worry about the future. Focus on what you can do on this 24-hour day.

God grant me the serenity to accept the things I cannot change the courage to change the things that I can and to know the difference.

NOTES

If you would like help with your car accident injury case, first review the copy below of the 100% Satisfaction Guarantee.

If that meets with your approval then call toll-fee
1-866-303-1411
to schedule an office appointment or a telephone conference with Mr. Hogan.

The Law Center for Car Accident Injuries

SAMPLE

Dan -

My Personal Promise to *You*

As a valued client I want you **100% SATISFIED** with your decision to hire me as your lawyer.

You should know within **90 DAYS** whether or not I am the ***right*** lawyer for you.

So, I offer you a

RISK-FREE PROMISE, NO QUESTIONS ASKED GUARANTEE!

If you are **NOT 100% SATISFIED** with my services you can fire me and

NOT OWE ME 1 PENNY!

CALL TOLL-FREE
1-866-303-1411

Paul Hogan, Attorney
Licensed in Kansas and Oklahoma

BONUS

THE TOP 10 CHECKLIST: THE TOP 10 ISSUES YOU NEED TO DEAL WITH **NOW**

Time has flown by since you were injured in a car accident. Life gets busy with doctors' appointments, raising kids, sometimes raising grandkids, work, physical therapy appointments and life's normal daily activities.

Here is my gift to you – time is precious in a busy life. Below is a list of issues taken from my exclusive checklist (one I prepared after decades of service helping over 10,000 people just like you, injured in a car accident).

No one is usually prepared for all that occurs when an unexpected car accident happens. I hope with this checklist in hand it can save you time by identifying those issues that need your attention ***now.***

1. You should have three (3), and possibly four (4), different claim numbers for your car accident:

    a. No Fault or Personal Injury Protection (PIP) claim number that you provide to your medical providers;

    b. Property damage claim number for auto repairs either through your insurance company if you have collision coverage or through the bad drivers insurance company;

    c. The Liability claim number for the bad driver/adverse drivers insurance coverage – this may be, and probably is, the same as the property damage claim number;

    d. The Uninsured (UM) claim number from *your* insurance company if the bad driver/adverse driver did *not* have insurance.

2. You should be receiving treatment for your injury(s) and should have obtained a doctor's written statement regarding your physical restrictions and/or inability due to injury to perform your job duties – you need to mail this doctor's statement to *your* PIP carrier;

3. You should have received your PIP application, provided the requested information and returned to your PIP carrier;

4. You should have obtained wage verification from your employer and mailed to your PIP carrier;

5. Your property/vehicle damage should be fixed or you have been paid the "fair market value" if your vehicle was *totaled*;

6. You should have obtained the records and bills from the medical providers for EMS, Emergency Room, Emergency Doctor (yes, it's separate from the ER Room bill), surgeons or specialists, radiologists and the hospital (if admitted);
7. Hopefully you have received your first wage loss check – if not contact your PIP carrier;

8. You need to keep a *written* log of the time, expenses, mileage and names of those who help you to do the things you cannot do now that you were able to do for yourself before the injury – such as laundry, cleaning house, grocery shopping, driving to doctors' appointments, etc. – these activities are known as *Essential Services.*

9. You need to send a copy of your Essential Service log to your PIP carrier with a demand for payment at $25 a day. NOTE: You'll also have to submit an updated doctors note stating your limitations each time you send in your log.

10. You need to WATCH THE DATE! Remember that in most cases you only have 2 years from the date of your accident to either settle your claims or file a law

suit. Please note that the time limitation date is different for minors and uninsured/underinsured cases.

My experience, again gleaned from almost 40 years of dealing with over 10,000 car accidents, is that insurance companies will delay or even worse – **deny** – payment when these issues stated above are ignored.

Read the next Bonus section, *Insurance Company Secrets Revealed: 66 Reasons Why Insurance Companies Delay, Diminish or DENY Your Claim* to learn the most common "lines" insurance companies will tell you so they don't have to pay you the money you deserve.

Extra BONUS

INSURANCE COMPANY SECRETS REVEALED: **66 REASONS WHY INSURANCE COMPANIES *DELAY, DIMINISH* OR *DENY* YOUR CLAIM**

Here's a list of 66 reasons used by insurance companies to delay, diminish or deny your claim. In a nutshell, it boils down essentially to two points.

1. You were not injured in this car accident, or it is so minor that it is of nuisance value and you are a crybaby.

2. If you WERE injured, it is either your fault, or someone else is at more fault than their insured.

They will try to discredit you, antagonize you, and make you feel like you are a bad person, because you are making a claim on their company. Their position is the car accident would not have happened if you had not been driving on that street at that time. Of course, you could reduce that argument down to the absurd -- if you had not been born, they would not have to deal with any this.

Here are reasons I've heard listening to 40 years of insurance adjusters telling me why they won't or can't pay money. Some I've gathered from other attorneys but most I've heard myself:

1. Your vehicle was not equipped with head rests, seatbelts, a rearview mirror or other safety device. It

is your responsibility to provide your vehicle with these devices.

2. Seatbelts or other safety devices were available in your vehicle, but you chose not to use them.

3. There was equipment defect in your vehicle such as bald tires, brakes not working, taillights not working, or turn signals not working.

4. Your driving ability and perception were impaired by the use of alcohol, medication or drugs.

5. You had hearing or visual defects and were not wearing your hearing aid or glasses.

6. You had other physical defects such as epilepsy, headaches, sickness or others which impaired your driving ability and perception.

7. You were under doctors' orders not to drive.

8. You are not licensed to drive or you are driving with a suspended license.

9. You did not notice the bad driver until impact, or immediately before impact, and therefore you were inattentive.

10. Your recollection of times, speeds, distances are so inaccurate as to indicate your inattentiveness or incompetence in driving and at the very least, diminishes your credibility.

11. You exaggerate the bad driver's speed and other facts surrounding the accident, so as to diminish your

credibility, which makes you unreliable or unbelievable as a witness.

12. You had warning of danger within a sufficient time to avoid the accident if you were paying attention.

13. You could've avoided the accident. If you had not been exceeding the safe speed for the conditions then existing.

14. You made an unnecessary and unexpected stop.

15. You made an unsafe lane change without signaling.

16. You did not give a stop or turn signal.

17. You were backing up under circumstances and/or at a location where reasonable persons would not have anticipated you, or where it was difficult for the bad driver to see you.

18. You were not in the intersection first.

19. If you and the bad driver are in the intersection at the same time. You were to the bad drivers left or exceeding the speed limit, a safe speed, or were inattentive.

20. You make a poor appearance as a witness.

21. You have verbal difficulty describing events surrounding the accident.

22. The bad driver was acting as "a reasonable person" in the operation of this vehicle including a safe speed, and therefore the bad driver was not negligent or at

fault, - the bad driver's actions were not the probable cause of the accident.

23. An act of God or an unknown person was responsible for the accident.

24. There is no independent witnesses who can substantiate your version of the accident (Nor can a witness be found). You have a legal duty to prove by a "preponderance of the evidence" each element of your claim/case.

25. There are witnesses who dispute your version of the facts or there are witnesses who substantiate the bad driver's version of the story.

26. The investigating police officer made errors in his report or erroneous conclusions disputing your version of the accident.

27. Physical evidence including lights, brakes, tires etc. was lost, and it was necessary to have it examined by an expert to substantiate your version of the facts.

28. You did not obtain the services of an expert to substantiate the negligence of other parties.

29. The police were not summoned to the scene thus confirming there was minimal or no injury.

30. There is no indication on the police report that you complained of pain at the scene of the accident.

31. There was no complaint of pain at the scene of the accident by you to anyone.

32. There are no objective signs of injury at the scene of the accident like cuts or bruises.

33. You made errors in recalling your medical and/or employment history to the bad driver's insurance company. This is later discovered by defense attorneys during litigation.

34. You do not have a medical opinion by a physician substantiating medical causation between the accident and your medical complaints.

35. Shortly after the accident, your physical/health condition returned to what it was immediately before the accident.

36. Before the accident, you had made complaints and received treatment to the same areas of your body, allegedly injured in the accident and your complaints after the accident had not changed.

37. After the accident, you had an injury/second accident which caused or continued your problems from the initial accident and you had no treatment between the first accident and the second.

38. You exaggerate complaints related to the accident, which is noted in your medical records.

39. Your complaints to your doctor were minimal.

40. Your complaints to your doctor were bizarre, exaggerated, and lengthy as contained in your medical records.

41. Your complaints to one doctor were different from your complaints to other doctor (s).

42. You had a full range of motion at a physical examination.

43. You had no complaint of pain at a physical examination.

44. You were observed moving normally, while not being examined by a doctor. (Upon arriving, in the waiting room or departing from the examination.

45. Your family doctor opinioned that your injuries were minimal, and he did not prescribe physical therapy or any other treatment, nor did he give you an appointment for you to return or tell you to "return in a month if you experienced pain". You did not see that doctor again.

46. Your injuries are totally "subjective" – there is no indication of injury from x-rays, orthopedic test or observation.

47. You received minimal treatment for a minimal time period after the accident.

48. Your doctor is no longer in the area or otherwise unavailable.

49. You are examined by a doctor recommended by the insurance company soon after the accident, and he determined you were not injured, and not in need of treatment.

50. You have chronic type complaints contained in your past medical records or you have an unrelated medical problem such as arthritis or congenital problems such as spondylosis.

51. Your cost of treatment is excessive, and the time during which you were treated was excessive in light of the standard charges for such services in the

community and for the normal time period of disability for such injuries.

52. You would work, contrary to your doctor's advice and you thereby aggravated your injury, and/or you caused a prolonged period of disability and/or treatment.

53. Your doctor did not recommend time off of work, and yet you took time off of work.

54. No doctor stated you would lose work time in the future.

55. You have poor attendance at work before the accident.

56. You would've been terminated, on strike, or laid off even without the accident.

57. You did not have a job at the time of the accident and you could not substantiate that you were applying at various places.

58. Your earnings on your W-2 and tax records indicate a smaller earning history than what you claim.

59. You were paid by cash for prior employment, and you cannot document past earnings and/or you have no tax returns.

60. Your claimed employer has no official record (i.e., W-2 forms) or other means to substantiate your claimed employment.

61. You have let various "statutes of limitations." run, thereby foreclosing possibility of recovering anything for your claim.

62. You are partially at fault and you should recover less under the comparative fault law of Kansas.

63. You have a history of filing lawsuits for the purpose of collecting compensation/money.

64. You have a history of mental illness or emotional problems, making you unreliable.

65. You gave a statement to the insurance company immediately after the accident that you were not injured in the accident.

66. You failed to give proper and timely notice to governmental entities or subdivision, and your claim is barred.

If you would like help with your car accident injury case,
first review the copy below of the
100% Satisfaction Guarantee.

If that meets with your approval then call toll-fee
1-866-303-1411
to schedule an office appointment
or a telephone conference with Mr. Hogan.

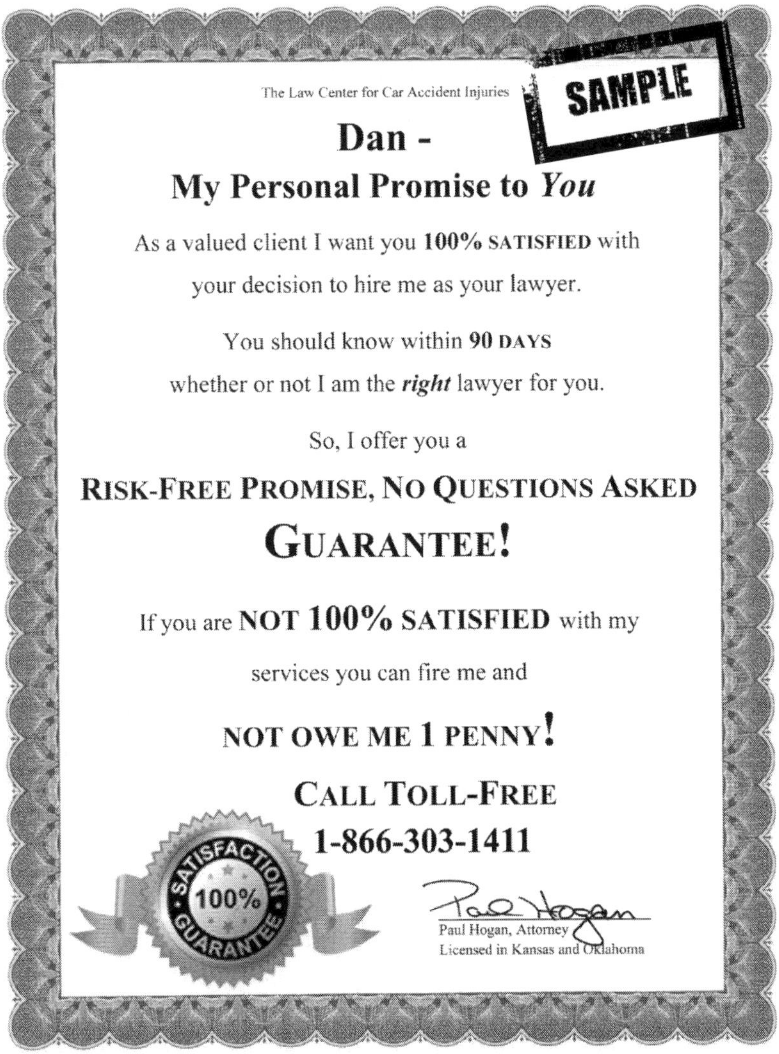

The Law Center for Car Accident Injuries

SAMPLE

Dan -

My Personal Promise to *You*

As a valued client I want you **100% SATISFIED** with
your decision to hire me as your lawyer.

You should know within **90 DAYS**
whether or not I am the ***right*** lawyer for you.

So, I offer you a

RISK-FREE PROMISE, NO QUESTIONS ASKED

GUARANTEE!

If you are **NOT 100% SATISFIED** with my
services you can fire me and

NOT OWE ME 1 PENNY!

CALL TOLL-FREE
1-866-303-1411

SATISFACTION 100% GUARANTEE

Paul Hogan, Attorney
Licensed in Kansas and Oklahoma

NOTES

ABOUT THE AUTHOR

Paul Hogan has practiced law for 38 years in Wichita, Kansas. Born in Ellsworth, Kansas, he was raised in Wichita, Kansas. After a stint in the Navy and Law School in Oklahoma, Paul chose to come home to Wichita. He lives with his wife, Cheri, and after raising two children now grown and on their own, he and Cheri share their home with Teddy, their enthusiastic goldendoodle.

Paul began exclusively handling car accident cases in the mid 1990's and has conferred with over 10,000 injured clients, actual and prospective. Over his career, Paul has obtained millions of dollars in recovery for his clients.

An Amazing 96% of Client's Surveyed
Would Recommend Paul to a
Friend or Family Member.

In the last two years of clients' surveyed Paul has not received less than a 10 (on a scale of 1-10, 10 being excellent) from *every single client* for excellence in customer service!

If you would like help with your car accident injury case,
first review the copy below of the
100% Satisfaction Guarantee.

If that meets with your approval then call toll-fee
1-866-303-1411
to schedule an office appointment
or a telephone conference with Mr. Hogan.

The Law Center for Car Accident Injuries

SAMPLE

Dan -

My Personal Promise to *You*

As a valued client I want you **100% SATISFIED** with your decision to hire me as your lawyer.

You should know within **90 DAYS** whether or not I am the ***right*** lawyer for you.

So, I offer you a

RISK-FREE PROMISE, NO QUESTIONS ASKED

GUARANTEE!

If you are **NOT 100% SATISFIED** with my services you can fire me and

NOT OWE ME 1 PENNY!

CALL TOLL-FREE
1-866-303-1411

Paul Hogan, Attorney
Licensed in Kansas and Oklahoma

13657569R00059

Made in the USA
San Bernardino, CA
31 July 2014